LANDSCAPES • COUNTRY LANES

VILLAGER JIM'S

PEAK DISTRICT

WILDLIFE AND FARM LIFE • GARDENS

LANDSCAPES • COUNTRY LANES

VILLAGER JIM'S

PEAK DISTRICT

WILDLIFE AND FARM LIFE • GARDENS

VP

Published by Vertebrate Publishing, Sheffield.
www.v-publishing.co.uk

LANDSCAPES • COUNTRY LANES

VILLAGER JIM'S
PEAK DISTRICT

WILDLIFE AND FARM LIFE • GARDENS

VP First published in 2015 by Vertebrate Publishing.
Vertebrate Publishing, Crescent House, 228 Psalter Lane, Sheffield S11 8UT, United Kingdom.

A CIP catalogue record for this book is available from the British Library.
ISBN: 978-1-910240-65-6 (Hardback)
10 9 8 7 6 5 4 3 2 1

Front cover: *Golden pheasant* – one of my-all time favourite pheasant shots (and yes, always shot with a camera – always!). The sun has
brought out how truly amazing this bird is. **Back cover**: (top left) Curbar in the morning mist; (top centre) *Bobbin* the robin poses for me
on an old wooden crate as she waits for me to feed her breakfast; (top right) I love looking at this photo, it just screams Old England;
(bottom) Foolow village, with morning mist behind and the rural checkerboard effect which I love so much in front.

All photography by Villager Jim.

VG Designed and typeset in The Sans, Glober and Swistblnk Monthoers by Nathan Ryder – www.v-graphics.co.uk

Vertebrate Publishing is committed to printing on paper from sustainable sources.

MIX
Paper from
responsible sources
FSC® C110418

Printed and bound in Slovenia by Latitude Press Ltd.

CONTENTS

FOREWORD

I guess you could almost call it a farm; it has at least always been a farm. The land has been in my family for generations, millennia even. We first moved here after the last Ice Age; we were immigrants, making our way from an overcrowded central Europe. We settled here in the high country; the forest was a little thinner, food was plentiful. Generations of us have lived and gathered on this farm, through harsh winters and through invasions, until today and my generation, my genes, my DNA. We are still farming in the same way as we have always done, even though it seems that with every generation the farm gets smaller and smaller, and the harvest meaner and meaner.

There has been some exciting news. We have a new tenant that helps with the farming; he's called Jim. He's taken a bit of time to train, but he's getting the hang of it. We have got him to plant a few more trees, we've taught him about the best time to cut the meadows, he helps with the harvest, and the farm is getting bigger again. He even gets up on time and joins in with the morning singing. That said, he still needs a bit more training; he is forever disappearing with his camera, seeing all the other tribes in the district, but he is usually back about lunchtime, which is good.

And there's something else that he is doing. He is telling other tenant people, with the help of his camera, about our farm, where we live, what we do and how they can help the farming district. I hear this is a good thing; his photographs are changing things – even my posh Chatsworth cousins are saying that.

So when he asked me to write a foreword for his book, because he wanted to tell the people about our Peak District farm, I said I would. And not just because he helps me out when it's cold or wet or I have too many mouths to feed, but because I quite like him. I like his photographs, I really like the house he built for us. I like what he is doing, and the other tribes seem to like him as well. He bumbles along a bit, living the village life, but we've had worse tenants. Maybe you'll like his book, it's even got a few pictures of me in it. And to think I don't even know his real name, we just call him Villager Jim.

Deidre Bluetit
Peak District farm – October 2015

Deidre. She's one in a million and one of my best friends in the garden. She'll sit on my feet or on my knee if I'm in the garden chair – she just stares at me intently and shouts: 'give me some more food Mr Jim!'

LANDSCAPES

Morning sunlight tears through mist and woodland near Calver.

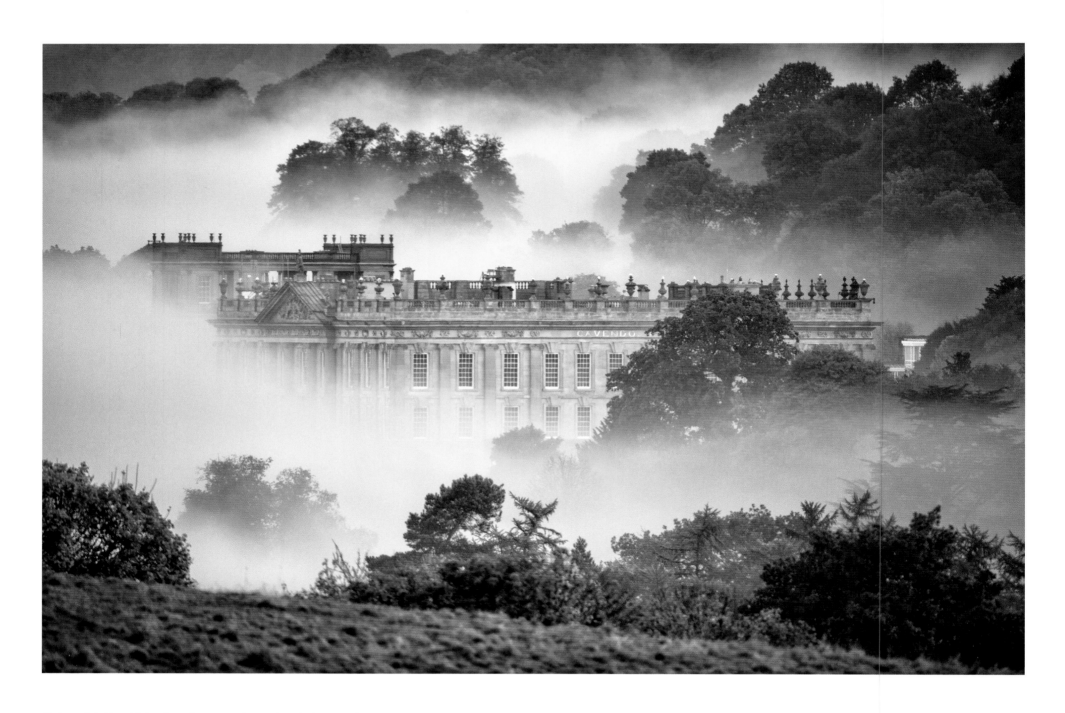

Chatsworth in the mist. An ethereal scene as mist envelops the house early one morning.

Mist drifts through Foolow on a cool October morning.

Deer shadows. A lovely moment: as I came round the corner at Chatsworth
these beautiful red deer were gracefully passing by the front of the house.

Deers at Chatsworth. Two young deer rut with the house at
Chatsworth making a rather nice backdrop.

River reflection. Chatsworth House is only four miles or so from my home so I am blessed with having the most photogenic house in England right on my doorstep.

Looking south towards the weir from the humpback bridge at Chatsworth.

Autumn gold. An old ruin resting by the River Derwent
between two stunning autumnal trees.

Misty cottage. I always think this house on the Chatsworth Estate
would make a dream home – a little slice of heaven.

Autumnal hues colour the landscape around Froggatt.

A lone cottage near the village of Crowdecote; another dreamland location to in live don't you think?

Monsal Head. The views from Monsal Head are lovely. If you visit the Peak District then please come here; have an ice cream, take the weight off your feet and enjoy the scenery.

Dry stone walls abound in the Peak District, making for great landscapes with contrast and colour.

Another misty morning in Foolow. Taken at midsummer on the lane to the Barrel Inn at Bretton (a great pint and lovely food!).

My neighbours' house, looking quite mystical, appears from
the morning mist as it drifts towards Litton.

My neighbours' house looking rather dramatic.

Barn flag. No matter how many times I look at this photo , I always see a flag!

This little barn above Bradwell is in such a lovely setting, with chequered fields and distant woodland.

Owl barn. I love this place, it is so dramatic! I love photographing it in all seasons and weather conditions.

Ashford in the Water – you simply *have* to visit this village.

The bridge at Ashford in the Water. Another view I love in different seasons.

One of my favourite trees, this one near Tideswell.

Sunrise above a farm at Beeley.

Thomas and *Bertie* pose perfectly in a February sunset.

Beeley Moor sunrise. One of the best places to be in the Peak District at this time of day; surrounded by wonderful wildlife, you have a view for miles of the rising sun.

Some snowdrifts! This small lane between the fields in Foolow takes the brunt of a major snow flurry.

Snow barn. My neighbours' barn looking amazing after a winter snowfall.

Bumble having a complete ball of a time with the lane completely blocked with snow.
OK, OK … and … me too!

This old quarry, now filled with water, looks so inviting. I will give my age away when I say that all I see when I look at this picture is one of those old public information adverts on TV before afternoon telly was invented!

The hills over Castleton look sensational with broken sunshine after rainfall – always a great time for lovely light!

This was a totally unique moment for me, and will go down as one of my most amazing wildlife experiences. In a spectacle known as a 'murmuration', this is a flock of starlings who have just left their roost at dawn on their daily travels – all exploding out into the countryside. When they spotted a fox on the ground they suddenly changed direction and headed for that lonely tree!

A freezing April morning at Ladybower, with beautiful reflections on the reservoir.

Poppies are my favourite flowers ... such emotion to them.

The outcrops of rock above Curbar are a fabulous location for climbers and are normally busy with people at weekends. I go there not for the climbing but for the stags that roam the moorland above the crag.

Bakewell, a beautiful market town near my home, is a magical place very early when no one is around. If you get chance to visit, try getting up at around 4.30 a.m. in the summer and walking round ... go on force yourself!

Eyam camper. Two of my favourite things; the Peak District and camper vans. This classic camper is owned by a musician from Manchester who comes to stay in his own field which he bought just for that purpose – I love that so much!

A tractor run going over the old Roman road at the top of
Sir William Hill above Eyam.

Streams and streams of tractors go by, each one totally different to the next.
I was grinning like a Cheshire cat.

There are a few trees along my journeys I've become attached to, and this is one of them near Bubnell.
I find they seem to change character with the passing of the seasons.

In March I spent a night in my new camper van and when I got up it was -2°, but upon leaving the campsite I came across this wonderful tree in the freezing morning mist.

Tree of life. Possibly my favourite tree of all – this one is on the Chatsworth Estate and is simply spectacular, especially in winter.

Another one of my favourite trees which is near Tideswell.
This picture was taken early one spring morning.

Tree of bronze. I don't really need to say much about this tree do I? Beautiful!

Two walkers enjoy a Christmas stroll by the River Derwent at Chatsworth.
This image was published in the *Daily Mail*.

A carpet of mist envelops Great Longstone. I took this photograph from one
of my favourite places – Longstone Edge.

COUNTRY LANES

Abney in autumn. The road to the gliding club above our home always looks fabulous in autumn.

What makes this image for me is the fact you can't actually see the driver and co-driver are smiling, but you just know they are! This one is full of joy.

Two wonderful eccentrics clattering down a country lane towards me near Baslow.

What makes this shot is the stern expressions on their faces.

... and off they go!

I wonder what he's saying ... 'did you see that weirdo with the camera?'

Coming home from a shoot one morning I decided to turn up past the Eyam Museum.
Just round the corner I came across this wonderful setting – I was so glad I made that detour!

Hassop is such a sleepy hamlet; it has a beautiful winding through road which goes
past the Eyre Arms pub where you'll get a great pint.

Morning mist swirls above Eyam.

A lane near Hope full of fantastic summer lushness.

Chocolate box cottages. Taken in my home village of Foolow in winter.

Chocolate box cottages. A summertime version of the cottages in Foolow.

Ashford in the Water. One of those streets you could be forgiven for thinking was stuck in the 1940s.

If you've never visited Ashford in the Water please do, its a stunning village thrown back in time.

An old Landy comes down our lane from Bretton in the winter snow.

A photo that looks as though it could have been taken forty years ago.

The barn a few yards down my lane, home to so much life. Little owls live here,
together with a kestrel and about 246 rabbits!

A dusting of fresh snow on a lane near Wardlow.

Autumn classic. This is a very poignant shot for me. This man drove by, waving and smiling at me as happy as can be. Afterwards I did some online research of his car to make contact so I could send him a free print, as I often do, only to find out that he had passed away the day after I had taken the shot. I sent his daughter the framed print as a good memory and received a beautiful letter by return.

This Tudor cottage near Chatsworth is another of those wonderful 'chocolate-box cottages'.

The Tour de France in Litton? Maybe rather hopeful, but you never know.

A tractor run of over ninety vehicles going through my home village.
Photographic heaven!

My good friend *Andrew* driving trusty old *Kermit*.

Old, trusted tractor *Kermit* – he looks so sad doesn't he?

Puddle House. (Not its *real* name – I called it Puddle House for the shot!) It's my favourite cottage on Earth, situated at the northern entrance to the Chatsworth Estate.

There are so many chocolate-box cottages in the villages of the Peak District. This is one of the most beautiful for sure – it's in the village of Parwich.

Do these chaps look happy? You can see from their faces they live a great life can't you!

One morning while travelling to Tideswell, I came across this young lady who seemed to think it was her right of way. Who was I to argue?

Three young deer casually crossing the lane near Curbar.

Another one of my favourite shots, taken near Parwich, as a pheasant ambles across a tree-lined avenue.

Let's get ready to rumble!

Summer mornings are the best times for me. Beautiful moments that I witness, like this young deer
crossing the road, are really special in a selfish 'was I the only one witnessing it?' way.
It's kind of wonderful, if you get me?

WILDLIFE AND FARM LIFE

Summer hares. For me the perfect photo description of an English summer.

Harry posing for me near Tideswell.

Harry is my favourite hare of all. He allows me just enough time to take shots – I swear he's got
used to my visits up the lane near Tideswell.

The local rabbits on my farm have a wonderful habit of sitting on top of the walls watching the world go by.

It's completely normal, but every time I see it I smile as it just looks so funny.

This little stunner was sitting on the road near the quiet village entrance to Great Hucklow.

This heron shot was taken in very low light at Bubnell weir.
The water, especially, has a chrome-like feel to it.

Henry the Heron who lives at Chatsworth. Although I see *Henry* a lot he's become a really
fun challenge for me because when I see him it's often when I can't lift my camera.
Henry is a real character – he knows he drives me crazy!

A dipper in the river by Monsal Head.

A young swan has a quick test of her amazing wings at the Sheepwash Bridge in Ashford in the Water.

Bathtime in Foolow for three of the forty-odd sparrows we have living in our trees. It really is an apartment block of them we have – such social birds yet also always wary of the local sparrowhawk.

A jackdaw near Monsal Head who, every day, proceeds to empty the bins of wrappers and cartons looking for his dinner.
He leaves a big mess that people always think is left by humans – little do they know it's this chap.

Two great spotted woodpeckers by the cattle grid just over the bridge at Chatsworth.

A meadow pipit with lunch for some hungry chicks – there were four of them just
six feet further down the wall.

Nest making. A wonderful meadow pipit collecting materials for making nests. She's readying herself for bringing up the new brood.

Meadow pipits can be found all around our farm and they are quite brave little chaps. They always seem to give me that extra second or so before they fly away, allowing me to get some nice shots.

A young kestrel goes into a high-speed dive while hunting a small field mouse at Great Longstone.

Evil eye. Sparrowhawks are truly amazing birds, but they're really unwelcome guests at my bird tables, which they treat like their own personal salad bars.

A truly wild stag leaps a dry stone wall near Curbar.

A young deer rests in the long summer grass at Chatsworth.

Two wild stags stand in the long grasses near Beeley Moor. Nothing gives me greater pleasure than taking shots of wild stags; they are simply magical creatures.

A once in a lifetime shot, taken one morning at Chatsworth. As this group of stags started to worry about a walker on the other side of the hill coming too close, one by one they got up. I was shaking as I photographed them as I realised that, incredibly, they all stood up in height order. Never again will I take a shot like this; it was a super-special moment and I was like a giddy kipper on the way home, singing and shouting to myself in the car – I must have looked bonkers!

The gentle beauty of a young female deer on top of a Derbyshire dry stone wall.

Brave little one. This one brave little dear came forward from the herd to inspect me – hats off to her; she had real heart.

A stunning tawny owl napping in the open in my neighbours' garden.

This guy doesn't like joking around – he's far too serious.

I love this shot – the moment just before take-off. Milliseconds later, with huge concentration, she took off and pounced on something in the field. As I watched her I saw she had actually pounced on ... wait for it ... a worm!

The same dozy-head from the previous spread who flew from my neighbours' house into our garden. She decided to sit on my garden chair and pose for me. I pray for moments like these and, every now and again, they happen.

Bubnell is a lovely village, and their local little owl sits in the morning sun below his favourite tree.

Little owls are such beautiful birds of prey. Just look at those eyes!

My favourite owl shot of all time. The question is; can you find her?

Barney, the village barn owl, out hunting in the day. Something he does quite regularly up and down the walls of my farm.

A hilarious moment. I came across this group of young stoats crossing, and playing on, the road.

Boing, boing, boing ...

... waiting for his brothers and sisters to catch up.

Roderick pops out of a bush to check out what he can pilfer.

Another magical moment as thousands of starlings came together to make the shape of a flying bird.

The moment I snapped it, I felt I had something very special.

Field pheasant. A crisp winter morning near Foolow and this young man showed me his true glory
with the most fabulous golden colours lit by the warm dawn sunlight.

Kung fu time for these two battling it out for the ladies.

Fighting pheasants. After much circling, which lasted many minutes, these two finally get it on in a flurry of two or three seconds before one of them decides it best to find his own turf.

A young fox is mobbed by a curlew as it runs too close to her nesting chicks.
The curlew was really harassing the fox until she finally made it run away.
Something I've never seen before and quite amazing to watch. Well done lass.

The beaten fox, not standing for any more harassment, beats a hasty
retreat over the wall to Great Hucklow.

Mr Fox gives himself away as he peeks out of the crop to gauge his location.

A curlew taking off from a rock face on one of my favourite lanes for wildlife near Tideswell.
It's also where *Harry* the hare lives too.

Curlew curves. One of my top-ten cherished shots that I've taken. With curlews and mist being two of my best-loved things to shoot, getting them both in one shot was an exquisite moment.

The curlew's call is hauntingly beautiful and it's so great to hear it each year when they come back to nest. If you haven't heard a curlew before, try to seek one out as it's such a magical sound – trust me.

Goofy pulling a wonderful expression for me. Her hairdo is so fantastic. Cows' hairdos are all
different and I urge you, next time you look at a cow close up, look at their hairdo –
you'll never look at a cow in the same way again.

Snotty cow. I do love cows. They have such wonderful expressions – and they're so inquisitive.

Three calves hoofing and racing around the field for no other reason than to play.

Best buddies. Two farmyard orphans – both mothers died and these two became totally inseparable, so much so that the farmer decided to keep them as pets!

Larry and *Buddy* have a serious friendship head-rub.

Check out that hairdo!

Hop, skip, jump. Full of the joys of spring, just look at that back kick!

There's always one isn't there? Stepping out of line, when will they learn?

Rolling Tommy. Thomas our horse is a special one, he's so good natured and genuinely thinks
he's a dog; he runs round with my labs and always runs up to them to say hello – I swear
he has watched them roll and then copied them.

A meadow full of buttercups creates a peaceful setting for this shot.

Thomas walking in our field full of buttercups. He's such a beautiful animal and has such a soft heart.

Zebra spotted in the wild near Bakewell.

Elvis smiling for mints. Elvis is another one of our fantastic horses and he has learned a trick. If he can smell mints and has an audience, without any coercion, he starts smiling. The more you laugh, the longer he does it – he knows he's performing. He's taught himself this trick which I always find amazing.

In my opinion *Thomas* is one of the best horses in the world – he's such a gentle chap and full of life. I fell asleep in our field with him once: he was on the floor, but with his eyes open, I walked up to within six or seven metres from him and lay down watching him. The next thing I knew I had nodded off. When I woke up, not knowing what planet I was on, he was right next to me snoring away. Magical!

Thomas showing everyone how tough and hard he is after a new horse arrives in the next field. It's so much fun to watch him whinny and strut his stuff. He's a total softie in real life which is what makes it so fabulous to watch.

Go *Thomas*, go! Yeehaw!

Thomas was lying down one morning after I finished one of my morning shoots. I couldn't see him moving; something worried me so I looked through my zoom lens. There wasn't a murmur. So, slightly panicked, I opened the gate – it creaked and still nothing. I ran over and got to him out of breath with my heart pounding. At this point he let out the loudest snore you've ever heard and I burst out laughing with utter relief. He woke up, lifted his head slightly, looked at me to say 'oh, hi Dad' and then put his head back down – and off he went, back to sleep. I took this shot right then. We love him so much.

Every day I drive past this chap he has a different expression on his face,
he really makes my day. Today it's Mr Aloof.

Wellington, our new cockerel.

One of our village-pond ducks having a quick wash and brush up.

Could you be a happier dog? Rounding up sheep at Wardlow.

Bo and *Maggi* – two adorable border collies.

Harry the hare is seriously gorgeous. I've become so attached to him as he seems to have got so much braver and allows me to get really close. He made me laugh out loud when I was taking this shot as he popped up to peek over the rock to check I wasn't *too* close.

GARDENS

Jenny wren, my smallest garden visitor, waits patiently on a pot outside my kitchen door for the breakfast I give her. Come rain or shine she's there and normally making the loudest tweeting noises – I'm still amazed at the size of her vocal chords for such a tiny bird.

Here's *Jenny* again. I know its not original, but the name has stuck! She's a wonderful bird and has been in our garden over three years and through some seriously tough winters. I try to make sure she gets enough food; she packs a serious set of vocal chords for something the size of a ping-pong ball let me tell you.

Jenny posing for me in midwinter. I feed her a breakfast of mealworms and
I'm pretty sure she's damn grateful!

Here's my local frog.

This chap lives in the stone trough I have in my front garden. It amazes me how he gets up there as it's at least four feet high!

The Great Mephisto! I love this one of *Bobbin* – I see a cape being unfurled
in theatrical style every time I look at this shot.

Bobbin again, a real character in our garden. Here she stands on the spade I had put down only five seconds earlier. She follows me round the garden waiting for her next meal.

Bobbin takes off from cloud-like snow.

Bobbin prepares for the local barn dance and perfects her moves.

One of my best shots of *Bobbin* by our pond in the dappled summer sunshine.

Starlings are so often overlooked as pesky little critters but if you look closely
they are truly stunning birds – and very intelligent too!

This shot of two starlings in our garden was selected as the winner from 50,000 entries in a competition on the BBC *Springwatch* programme. A very proud moment indeed!

Four fledgling starlings sit tight while mum pops away for more food – a never-ending job with this lot.

A honeybee in our garden. This shot made the front page header for the
BBC Wildlife website, which made me rather proud.

A lovely bumblebee visits our garden. We named our dog *Bumble* as she also has a huge fat backside!

Betty, my favourite blackbird, poses as she waits for her breakfast.

Betty feeding one of her chicks only three feet away from me, just outside my kitchen door.

Betty has a shouting match with two local sparrows over the mealworm breakfast on our garden gate.

As I sat in our garden with my camera near my bird tables, this young sparrow decided to join me,
less than ten feet away, and promptly used a half-coconut feeder as a hammock!
She sat there, incredibly, for over an hour.

Two beautiful sparrows debate how the spade works as they've seen me bringing up worms with it in the past.

The queue for breakfast in our garden.

Barn dancing is a popular pastime where I live.

A young bullfinch pops by to see if he can grab some sunflower seeds from my table.

Our garden is blessed with over twenty or so goldfinches, one of the most beautiful of all garden birds.

This gorgeous little mouse sits inside a small flowerpot which I had put bird seed into.

What amazes me is how on Earth he found the food when it was on a three-foot pole!

Another one of my cherished shots. I watched him climb the pole and then proceed to eat all the bird seed inside the pot. He then gave me a magical moment by plonking his tail over the edge! I was laughing as I took this.

Congo in her favourite place – a pot ... stop those horrid jokes right now!

Ricky and his girls. Ricky our cockerel proudly guarding *Pongo* and *Perdita*.

Ricky and Tikka. Ricky is such a beautiful bird, and he cares very much for his ladies. When he finds food in the garden he always lets them feed first before he eats. Here he puts his arm round *Tikka* and checks out if the coast is clear.

Ricky and *Tikka* out for an afternoon stroll and chinwag.

I love this shot of these four – it reminds me of an action movie poster.

Tikka posing on our garden table.

Puss in roots. She was mid-hunt when I took this. Can you see the look on her face – if looks could kill, eh?

A stunning specimen in Great Longstone posing on a dry stone wall.

Valentino and *Bobo* nuzzle up together – they're totally devoted to each other.

Barnaby, my dog, looking at me through the pond grass. He's in the middle of the pond here and he's not allowed in, but I guess you can tell that from his face.

Round robin. This is one of my most popular robin images: with *Bobbin* standing by my feet looking
up at me with such professional cuteness how can I refuse to feed him?

Deidre's gone potty.

Deidre posing by her own private pool ready to do a swallow dive … err, is that right?

Deidre is either huge or it's a very small pot – you decide.

Deidre giving me the evils as she waits for her tin of mealworms to be handed over.
Here she sits on a wall on my drive staring at me through the car window.
I always feed her after I return from my morning shoot.

Deidre comes in to land on my wife's hand for her early morning breakfast.

Deidre popping by to say hello outside our kitchen on a warm spring morning.
Can I ask you, is there any more to life you could wish for?

A bird in the hand is worth a hell of a lot to me!

Follow Villager Jim's daily adventures on Facebook **f** VillagerJim

www.villagerjimsshop.com

Pop in for a browse and see the full range of products

CHOPPING BOARDS

TRAYS

PHONE COVERS

CUSHIONS

PLACEMATS & COASTERS

TABLET COVERS

CALENDARS

2016 CALENDAR
CHATSWORTH

2016 CALENDAR
PEAK DISTRICT

MUGS

NOTEBOOK

NOTEBOOK

NOTEBOOKS

UMBRELLAS

GREETING CARDS

www.villagerjimsshop.com

Naked man. The bloody cheek(s) of it!

LANDSCAPES • COUNTRY LANES

VILLAGER JIM'S

PEAK DISTRICT

WILDLIFE AND FARM LIFE • GARDENS